LEADERSHIP
GONE ROGUE

Published by:

EMPOWER ME BOOKS, INC.
A Subsidiary of Empower Me Enterprises, Inc.
P.O. Box 16153 Durham, North
Carolina 27704
www.EmpowerMeBooks.com

Scriptures marked NCV are ERV are taken from the HOLY BIBLE: EASY-TO-READ VERSION ©2014 by Bible League
International. Used by permission.

Scriptures marked KJV are taken from the KING JAMES VERSION (KJV): KING JAMES VERSION, public domain.

Scriptures marked NCV are taken from the NEW CENTURY VERSION (NCV): Scripture taken from the NEW CENTURY VERSION®. Copyright© 2005 by Thomas Nelson, Inc. Used by permission. All rights reserved.

Scripture taken from the Holy Bible, New International Version®, NIV®. Copyright ©1973, 1978, 1984, 2011 by Biblica, Inc.® Used by permission. All rights reserved.

Scriptures taken from Holy Bible, New Living Translation, NLT®. Copyright © 1996, 2004, 2015 by Tyndale House Foundation. Used by permission of Tyndale House Publishers, Inc., Carol Stream, Illinois 60188. All rights reserved.

ISBN: 978-1732773189

Printed in the United States of America

LEADERSHIP GONE ROGUE

DR. FREDRICK J. HARRIS

Leadership Gone Rogue

DEDICATION

LaKendra,
my love and life partner, who makes my life fun
and easy.
I love you.

Marquez, Christian, and Marley;
you are awesome young men who give me
strength.

ACKNOWLEDGMENTS

To Without Limits Ministries International
(W.L.M.I.), and all Covenant Friends and
Partners, both Lady Lakendra and I
appreciate your family's prayers and support
during this book's scribing.

FOREWORD

Proverbs 29:2 states, "When the righteous are in authority, the people rejoice: but when the wicked bear rule, the people mourn." Whether it be good or bad, leadership affects everyone. On the job, in governmental institutions, in military service, in ministry, in business, and the home, righteous leadership opens the door for growth, creativity, and joy. When wicked people are leaders, growth is stagnant, creativity is not valued, and joy is replaced with a toxic spirit.

Leadership is a spirit that is all about mindsets and attitudes. Leadership reveals an individual's true heart because it affords one more freedom and opportunity to exercise the will. In some instances, this freedom exercise has no consequences; this is why the practice of leadership in the wrong hands can bring much suffering.

Dr. Harris' analysis of *Leadership Gone Rogue* is a must-read for all leaders, followers, and those who desire to be good leaders. His book will challenge your thinking, attitude, and mindset. As you read this book, be open and willing to make the adjustments necessary to improve your leadership acumen.

The principles that he provides can be applied in any realm of society. Many people in positions of leadership are leaders in title only, but not in spirit. Many people have been elevated to leadership in the workplace, with no formal leadership training, simply because of their knowledge of a subject. This is a recipe for a potential disaster. Ministries have been destroyed, businesses have remained grounded, and talented employees have walked away from jobs because of knowledgeable yet incompetent leadership.

Dr. Harris and I have trained many leaders in ministerial service. One of the things we have always taught future leaders is that the time to prepare and grow in the spirit of leadership is now. Work on your leadership skills in your private time and obscurity. It is too late to study leadership administration once you are appointed because your followers' lives are on the line and deserve godly and righteous leadership from you. A plethora of rogue leaders have never taken the time to train and learn the principles of leadership.

Learn the principles of leadership now! Use this book, Rogue Leadership, as a training tool to help you grow in the spirit of leadership.

Dr. Randy Bell Sr.
Apostle, Zoe Life
Ministries Marietta,
Georgia

INTRODUCTION

This book will discuss the complexities of leadership. From the marketplace, military, ministry, and home life, there are major issues in leadership and those entrusted with great responsibility. The normal that we are witnessing is to lie until it sounds like truth for people to believe. God did not intend for humanity to become, but it is an unfortunate state of circumstance portrayed worldwide.

I will offer a question on this topic, what happened to authentic leadership? Are we so far gone that anything acceptable now just because it seems right and truthful? Have we become desensitized to allowing leaders in positions of power to say and do whatever they desire without accountability?

There are severe problems in America. We are in a place of complete dysfunction because of deception and lies from our government leaders and multiple facets of leadership that display ignorance as a way of acceptance. I am appalled that there is no clergy leadership standing up to the tensions that have brought condemnation upon the church in many religions and denominations. Who will be a voice for the people who do not understand the meaning of fighting back?

From my perspective, through interviews, group studies, symposiums, and church events, several people have expressed deep concern about our present leadership and those that will follow in the years to come. To stay engaged and connected with pertinent issues that plague our society today, you must love the facts and not the fascination of lies. It's so overwhelming that many have become immune to what is happening across multiple spectrums in our Nation. As a citizen and veteran of combat tours in Iraq and Afghanistan, I plan to utilize the voice God has given me to empower people for understanding and bring wisdom using God's word for insight and revelation to help His people awaken to the truth.

My prayer is for anyone reading this book to take the opportunity, have an open perspective, and see the revelation of God's word unfold to enlighten our insight that we have leaders who went rogue through the love of power and control over people.

John 8:8-10 (NLT)
All who came before me were thieves and robbers. But the

true sheep did not listen to them. Yes, I am the gate. Those who come in through me will be saved. They will come and go freely and will find good pastures. The thief's purpose is to steal and kill and destroy. My purpose is to give them a rich and satisfying life.

TABLE OF CONTENTS

CHAPTERS

Definitions used in this literary work have been derived from

the following sources: Merriam - Webster,

Military

Combat

Experience,

And some

Acronyms are from Military Combat experience or

are scribed, as provided and governed by the

Holy Spirit.

DEN of THIEVES

Rogue- A dishonest or unprincipled man.

In our society, the criminal justice system is utilized as a barometer to deter people from committing crimes and violent acts. However, over the last 30 years, America's illegal activity is not based solely on physical violence against another human.

Criminals today are more sophisticated in their approach to illegal activities of various kinds. The information source that reflects an individual's behavior comes from events introduced before the actual crime happened.

The word *rogue* is defined in this way: An elephant or other large wild animal driven away or living apart from the herd and having savage or destructive tendencies. This a compelling description, especially the statement about destructive tendencies.

Have we become susceptible to a society that forces upon us violent and dangerous tendencies? I have observed this behavior being unleashed in more manipulative and deceptive ways and causes people to be lured away and destroyed for lack of knowledge. Now is the time we, as Christians, should stay planted in God at all costs.

Ephesians 6:10-12 (NLT)

A final word: Be strong in the Lord and his mighty power. Put on all of God's armor so that you will be able to stand firm against all strategies of the devil. For we are not fighting against flesh-and-blood enemies, but against evil rulers and authorities of the unseen world, against mighty powers in this dark world, and against evil spirits in the heavenly places.

Churches are not exempt from these heinous attacks that have infiltrated the house of God. Major size congregations to the smallest congregations, I have seen the travesty onslaught that has come to paralyze movement for some churches.

Why is this happening in churches and our

2

government? Well, you always hear the quote, "never mix church & state." There is a bit of truth to this statement. However, when you look in the book of Revelation, God's word gives us a clear distinction of this prophecy and the peril we are facing today, and there is a depiction of this mistrust in the book of I Samuel 8.

Revelation 3:15-19 (NLT)
I know all things you do, that you are hot nor cold. I wish that you were one or the other! But since you are lukewarm water, neither hot nor cold, I will spit you out of my mouth!

You say, 'I am rich. I have everything I want. I don't need a thing!' And you don't realize that you are wretched and miserable and poor and blind and naked. So, I advise you to buy gold from

me- gold that has been purified by fire. Then you will be rich. Also, buy white garments from me so you will not be shamed by your nakedness, and ointment for your eyes so you will be able to see. I correct and discipline everyone I love. So be diligent and turn from your indifference.

I Samuel 8:6-9 (NLV)
But Samuel was not pleased when they said, "Give us a king to rule over us," And Samuel prayed to the Lord. The Lord said to Samuel, "Listen to the voice of the people in all they say to you, for they have not turned away from you.

3

They have turned away from Me, that I should not be king over them. They are doing to you what they have done since the day I brought them out of Egypt until now. They have turned away from Me and worshiped other gods. So, listen to their voice. But tell them of the danger and show them the ways of the king who will rule over them."

I have learned a vital lesson over the years, to let people make their own decisions regardless of the advice that will help them avoid trouble. Here are a few principles to understand when you are dealing with a den of thieves.

Daniel 6:16 (NCV)
So, King Darius gave the order, and Daniel was brought in and thrown into the lions' den. The king said to Daniel, "May the God you serve all the time save you."

    A. Pray- you must have a faithful and strong prayer life.
    B. Entrapment- stay away from the law of entanglement.
    C. Confusion- free yourself from any confusion and chaos.
    D. Angels- God will send angels to protect you and what you say.
    E. Trust- Never lose your identity of trust in the Lord.
    F. Peace- Orchestrate the peace you desire.

G. Honor- Always honor the Lord in all things.

H. Integrity- Do not undervalue your integrity for a quick fix.

History now is in a polarizing time that it is overwhelming to keep up with the rapid changes to circumstances. It looks as though there is trouble on every side. You must not negotiate with your future and give up on the dreams that are deep within. Even though we have issues and problems in our culture and nation, we must never relent to evil pressures to stop doing what is right. Deal with any issues completely and with honesty, leave the rest thieves in the hands of God.

UNFIT for DUTY

Unfit:

1. (of a thing) not of the necessary quality or standard to meet a particular purpose.

2. (of a person) not in good physical condition, typically as a result of failure to exercise regularly.

Verb
Make (something or someone)
unsuitable; disqualify.

Serving in the military for 26 years has taught me valuable lessons about life and responsibility. I held leadership positions during my tenure. Before working in any Leadership role, this question was always asked, "Do you believe you are fit for this position"?

During the interview process, I knew they were asking me about my physical fitness, mental wellness, and competence to lead? I knew the difference between this responsibility, and I believe this contrasts with many people who occupy leadership positions. They do not possess the competence for the leadership role. I was under several leaders who were not fit for leadership. Just because they knew someone or had the rank, they advanced to a position without any regard for experience or competence.

I remember in each vital leadership position; I had a tremendous responsibility because of the lives I would impact. There was great trust from my subordinate soldiers that the decisions I was empowered to make were putting them in the best position possible for success.

As a Senior NCO (Non-Commissioned Officer), you lived by the Creed of the NCO: The guideline and declaration. There are two main responsibilities in this creed:

1. The accomplishment of my mission. The welfare of my soldiers.

Creed:

1. A brief, authoritative formula of religious beliefs.
2. A set of fundamental beliefs, also a guiding principle.

I Samuel 14:6 (NLT)

"Let's go across to the outpost of those pagans," Johnathan said to his armor bearer. "Perhaps the Lord will help us, for nothing can hinder the Lord. He can win a battle whether he has many warriors or only a few!"

Duty or obligation refers to what one feels bound to do. Duty is what one performs, or avoids doing, in fulfillment of the permanent dictates of conscience, piety, right, or law: duty to one's country: one's duty to tell the truth.

Duty:

1. A moral or legal obligation; a responsibility.

2. A task or action that someone is required to perform.

3. A payment levied on the import, export, manufacture, or sale of goods.

4. The measure of an engine's effectiveness in units of work done per unit of fuel.

Leaders in the Church:

Church Leaders or Leadership is an extension of discipleship. It calls for Christians who are committed to increasing their leadership skills and deepening their spiritual practices.

Nehemiah 10:28-29 (NLT)

Then the rest of the people-the priests, Levites, gatekeepers, singers, temple servants, and all who had separated themselves from the pagan people of the land in order to obey the Law of God, together with their wives, sons, daughters, and all who were old enough to understand joined their leaders and bound themselves with an oath. They swore a curse on themselves if they failed to obey the Law of God as issued by his servant Moses. They solemnly promised to carefully follow all the commands, regulations, and decrees of the LORD our Lord.

The principle law is declared by many leaders who lead, preach, teach, and counsel God's word to His people and congregations. However, we have witnessed so much corruption, lies, manipulation, and deception among people trusting these types of leaders to care for their spiritual well-being.

<u>My Testimony</u>:

I served in a ministry for 15 years, and I was loyal and dedicated to helping the church and ministry in whatever capacity I could. For many years I believed in my pastor and spiritual leaders. I was young in my early twenties and wanted to learn and grow more in God. To my lack of understanding at that time, none of my spiritual training or elevations took place in this ministry. I knew there was a prophetic call on my life, but I had no assistance to guide me in wisdom.

I continually reached out to leadership, but there was no response to help me. I continue to send tithes and offerings to the ministry even though there was no help concerning my calling. I wanted answers, but the leaders were not available in any capacity. During my journey, God allowed others to cultivate my spiritual development.

From a chaplain in the U.S. Army to several men and women of God who took time to train and mentor me. But my loyalty and love were still with this ministry, and I continued to send financial support and tithes and offerings. Then things started frustrating me about this ministry, and here is what happened to change my focus. During the time I was deployed to Iraq, I was going through a dark time. I did not know that the next five years would be times of peaks and valleys for me. I tried to contact them for prayer and for the ministry to send me a care package to Iraq. I got no correspondence from them, and I was also dealing with my mother's illness and surgery. I figured they would visit my mother and offer prayer to my family. However, to my disappointment, outreach was not extended to my family.

During this challenging time came another tragedy. My brother passed away suddenly, and I thought then I would hear from the pastor. There was nothing, so now was trying to walk away from this ministry, but I was looking for validation and support and never received it. Things continued getting worse for me, and I am still holding out hope they would be there for me, but I was wrong. I went through a terrible divorce, and then following, my father passed away, and I deployed to Afghanistan. Thinking, surely now they would be there for me, but there was no communication of any kind.

With all, this was now the place I received my deliverance.

I started attending prophetic school years earlier, and simultaneously I was working on achieving my master's degree. Next, I pursued higher education for a doctorate, and I was elevated by God and affirmed before man into the office of an Apostle.

An apostolic council of Apostles met me and encouraged me to attend their school training for the Apostleship. I returned to my hometown for my affirmation and ordination, and I decided to stop by the ministry I used to attend. I stayed for the services, and afterward, the pastor asked me how things were in my life. I began to tell him, and he interrupted me to let me know that the council of apostles had contacted him about me. He then proceeded to tell me this statement, "I could not touch what God had done."

This quote from him released me from years of frustration and regret. On that day, I asked God for the forgiveness of all that I had harbored in my heart that God was using to educate me for ministry later in life.

So, I made it my quest to empower people with insight and information to support their goals and dreams to do God's will without frustration and animosity.

God has allowed me the incredible privilege of planting several churches, establishing prophetic academies, several schools for apostles and prophets, and a life coach training center. These are just the tip of the sphere in the vision that He has given me.

I could not get to this place without first going through hardships and disappointments. All praise, honor, and glory belong to the Lord.

Government Leadership, Politicians, and Military Leaders:

The political and military spectrum is challenging to harness all at the same time. Serving as a career soldier and studying political science in school, I have been waiting patiently for my opportunity to speak on things that I endured and witnessed during my military career and the destruction happening in our government by rude and selfish political leaders.

I served with and under some incompetent leaders and sacrificed so much energy and time to fix problems created by these leaders who had no idea what they were doing. Many of them were inferior because I displayed high moral character to accomplish assigned tasks, and I did not take a short cut to get it done. There were many instances where you saw the double standard method used to get over, and now the same is unfolding in our government today.

I watched the scope of tribalism being displayed by elected officials at the highest levels. And we are witnessing the number of scandals that plague our television screens and social media columns every day for the past two-plus years. As a veteran, I can surely say this is madness in full effect, and to watch the massive coverups taken place is a sheer spectacle and does not embody who we are as a people in the United States of America. We are witnessing the institutions that hallmark our democracy eroded by a man who does not know how to lead.

When your resume speaks of failure after failure, then this a red flag that someone should question such a person's moral competency who represents a spirit of a narcissistic nature. And this is not our normal, and I am pretty sure the framers of the U.S. Constitution did not have this behavior in mind.

This person has no political, military, or governmental experience and ascended to our country's most prestigious position. Wow, nobody sees an issue with how this happened? Where are the accountability and the integrity to do a vetting process on someone who is not fit for duty?

I Samuel 8:7-22 (ERV)
> *The Lord said to Samuel, "Listen to the voice of the people in regard to all that they say to you, for they have not rejected you, but they have rejected Me from being king over them. Like all the deeds which they have done since the day that I brought them up from Egypt even to this day- in that they*

15

have forsaken Me and served other gods- so they are doing to you also. Now then, listen to their voice; however, you shall solemnly warn them and tell them of the procedure of the king who will reign over them.

So, Samuel spoke all the words of the Lord to the people who had asked of him a king. He said, "This will be the procedure of the king who will reign over you: he will take your sons and place them for himself in his chariots and among his horsemen and they will run before his chariots. He will appoint for himself commanders of thousands and of fifties, and some to do his plowing and to reap his harvest and to make his weapons of war and equipment for his chariots. He will also take your daughters for perfumers and cooks and bakers. He will take the best of your fields and your vineyards and your olive groves and give them to his servants. He will take a tenth of your seed and of your vineyards and give it to his officers and to his servants. He will also take your male servants and your female servants and your best young men and your donkeys and use them for his work. He will take a tenth of your flocks, and you yourselves will become his servants. Then you will cry out in that day because of your king whom you have chosen for yourselves, but the LORD will not answer you in that day. "The Lord told Samuel, "Do what the people tell you. They have not rejected you, but they have rejected me. They don't want me to be their king, instead they are doing the same thing they have always done. I took them out of Egypt, but they left me and served other gods. They are doing the same to you. So, listen to the people and do what they say. But give them a warning. Tell the people what a king will do to them. Tell them how a king rules people.

Those people asked for a king. So, Samuel told them everything the LORD said. Samuel said, "If you have a king ruling over you, this is what he will do: He will take away your sons and force them to serve him. He will force them to be soldier- they must fight from his chariots and become horse soldiers in his army. Your sons will become guards running in front of the king's chariot.

"A king will force some of your sons to plow his fields and gather his harvest. He will force some of your sons to make weapons for war and to make things for his chariots.

"A king will take your daughters and force some of them to make perfume for him and some to cook and bake for him.

"A king will take your best fields, vineyards, and olive groves. He will take them from you and give them to his officers. He will take one-tenth of your grain and grapes, and he will give them to his officers and servants.

"A king will take your men and women servants. He will take your best cattle and your donkeys. He will use them all for his own work. He will take *one-tenth of your flocks. "And you yourselves will become slaves of this king. When that time comes, you will cry because of the king you chose. But the LORD won't answer you at that time."*

But the people would not listen to Samuel. They said, "No, we want a king to rule over us. Then we will be the same as all the other nations. Our king will lead us. He will go before us and fight our battles."

Samuel listened to the people and then repeated their words to the LORD. The LORD answered, "Listen to them and give them a king."

Then Samuel told the Israelites, "You will have a king. Now go home." Nevertheless, the people refused t listen to the voice of Samuel, and they said, "No, but there shall be a king over us, that we also may be like all the nations, that our king may judge us and go out before us and fight our battles. Now after Samuel had heard all the words of the people, he repeated them in the LORD's hearing. The LORD said to Samuel, "Listen to their voice and appoint them a king." So, Samuel said to the men of Israel, "Go every man to his city."

This scripture text is a prophetic proclamation that is being fulfilled right now in this hour. The political atmosphere is toxic and divided; the American people are in the crossfire of greed snipers that have swept across the country over the last two years. It is polarizing to witness such disasters happening that those who are blinded by the fiasco thinks it is

18

a laughable situation.

I am confident that the Bible will be fulfilled. It is up to us who mature spiritually to intercede and pray because of the onslaught of demonic activity that has covered this country. As a veteran, I cannot just sit on the sidelines and watch my brothers and sisters-in-arms who need access to premium healthcare. People are being turned away because of inexperienced people who are given in trusted positions like secretaries and have no idea what they are doing. That resembles poor and dysfunctional leadership. Now an all-time negative impact on future generations because of the foundation planted with discord and the inability to lead in times of crisis and peril.

Micah 6:9-12 (NLT)
> *Fear the LORD if you are wise!*
> *His voice calls to everyone in Jerusalem:*
> *"The armies of destruction are coming; the Lord is sending them.*
>
> *What shall I say about the homes of the wicked filled with treasures gained by cheating?*
> *What about the disgusting practice of measuring out grain with dishonest measures?*
> *How can I tolerate your merchants who use dishonest scales and weights?*
>
> *The rich among you have become wealthy through extortion and violence.*

Your citizens are so used to lying that their tongues can no longer tell the truth.

Reading the word of God and meditation day and night will cause you to begin experiencing the scales falling off. (Acts 9:18) You start to grow in your understanding, and now you have more questions than you ever had before because you are becoming progressive about your livelihood and how politics has shaped our country for decades. I am old enough now to receive knowledge and discern how these decisions are made by impulse and not the spirit of God, which enables such choices.

The spirit of greed, power, and influence are the driving components of erratic behavior from political leaders for their egregious ambitions, and the people are the ones that suffer the most.

That is why in this hour, we must have true prophets of God who are willing to stand for truth and not entertainment and let them know that the voice of God is speaking, so prepare to listen.

Ezekiel 2:1-10 (ERV)
The voice said, "Son of man, stand up and I will speak with you."
Then the Spirit came into me and lifted me up on my feet, and I listened to the one who spoke to me. He said, "Son of man, I am sending you to speak to the family of Israel. Those people and their ancestors turned against me many times. They have sinned against me many times-and they are

20

still sinning against me today. I am sending you to speak to them, but they are very stubborn. They are very hardheaded, but you must speak to them. You must say,

'This is what the Lord God says.' They are people who refuse to obey, so they may not listen to you. But even if they don't stop sinning, at least they will know that there is a prophet living among them.
"Son of man don't be afraid of the people or what they say. It is true: they will turn against you and try to hurt you. Their words will be sharp like thorns and will sting like scorpions. But don't be afraid of what they say. They are people who refuse to obey, but don't be afraid of them. You must tell them what I say, whether they listen or not.

They are people who usually refuse to listen!

"Son of man listen to what I am telling you. Don't turn against me like those people who refuse to obey. Now open your mouth to receive the words I will give you to speak.
Then I saw an arm reach out towards me. It was holding a scroll with words written on it. It rolled the scroll open in front of me. Words were on the front and on the back of the scroll. There were all kinds of sad songs, sad stories, and warnings.

These are all truths that are happening now in the three phases I have identified. Some principles could lead to true discipleship if they listen.

Lessons of Discipleship:

A.   Patience- dealing with difficult people is required (II Timothy 2:24)

B.   Encouragement- devote time to help others (Colossians 4:6)

C.   Wisdom- help save lives with wisdom (Proverbs 12:6)

D.   Compassion- exhibit concern in the process (I Peter 2:10)

E.   Obligation- answer the command to serve (Ecclesiastes 8:2)

F.   Duty- execute the mission (Matthew 18:15)

G.   Revelation- share the insight to remove yokes (Isaiah 10:27)

H.   Evangelize- share the good news of Jesus (I Timothy 1:5)

THE VETTING PROCESS

There is a structure to anything in life that has significance. Thus, there must be a process to streamline any activity that will cause some type of protocol to be established. Whether it is in the business community, serving in trusted positions in the military, or elected for political office, you must have a vetting system to activate transparency.

Vetting:
> The process of carefully and critically examining information or something to make an informed decision.

The process of a background investigation ensures the candidate is suitable for the position requiring secrecy, loyalty, and or trustworthiness. Also, conferring degrees, awards, and all additional fact checking before making any decisions.

Mathew 16:1,4 (NLT)

One day the Pharisees and Sadducees came to test Jesus, demanding that he show them a miraculous sign from heaven to prove his authority.

Only an evil, adulterous generation would demand a miraculous sign of the prophet Jonah. Then Jesus left them and went away.

We, the people of God, citizens of this country, are being challenged by several goliaths that have inserted themselves into our way of life. My hope is for people to be enlightened and aware of the malicious actions attacking the church, communities, and the institutions that govern our ability to have the freedoms and liberties that we enjoy. In many countries, this privilege is unheard of and is led by dictators and tyranny. It's unfortunate to see the suffering that many people are under because they voted for leaders who were never appropriately vetted. Many of these rogue leaders have killed and stolen their way to seize these countries' power and control.

John 10:10 (NLT)
The thief's purpose is to steal and kill and destroy. My purpose is to give them a rich and satisfying life.

Goliath:

1. In the Bible, a giant Philistine warrior was slain by David with a stone and sling.

2. A person or thing of colossal power or achievement.

I Samuel 17:4 (NLT)
Then Goliath, a Philistine champion from Gath, came out of the Philistine ranks to face the forces of Israel. He was over nine feet tall.

Looking into this scripture text, Goliath represents power and continues to hover over people in a taunting manner. Whether it is the pressures of daily life and responsibilities to studying midterm exams in college, you must handle a goliath in the way God would expect you to stand up and for victory because He strengthens you in battle.

As a believer, you must remain strong and vigilant to complete the task that God has given you.

Nobody told you it would be easy, but you must demonstrate patience and the willingness for great things will happen because of your obedience to the Lord.

I have learned this stringent principle of obedience, and it is not to be taken lightly. God is watching you, and He expects the best of you to come forward with power and grace.

Isaiah 1:19 (NIV)
> *If you are willing and obedient, you will eat the good things of the land.*

Zechariah 2:3(NIV)
> *Seek the Lord, all you humble of the land, you who do what He commands. Seek righteousness, seek humility; perhaps you will be sheltered on the day of the Lord's anger.*

Romans 3:21(NIV)
> But now apart from the law the righteousness of God has been made known, to which the Law and the Prophets testify.

Joel 2:21(NIV)
> Do not be afraid, land of Judah; be glad and rejoice. Surely the Lord has done great things!

PROPHETIC DECREE:

The Lord has done great things and will continue

to do great things! He is sending rain to harvest your soul and replenish your fields. In this hour, there a grace that is upon your life for great things. Be in anticipation of expedited increase from an open portal that gazes across the land just for you. Now rejoice and be glad, for the Lord is doing great things. The shower of praise is here, and the Lord is doing great things! The land with milk and honey awaits your arrival to usher you into the sweet fragrance of power that has been adorned for you and your household.

God says, "Prepare now for this fragrance. The pleasure and release of this smell confirm the answer and independence of the growth of your future. The season of waiting is over, reach up and take hold of the movement of this God-given fragrance that will increase in your spirit to all things God called you to do."

Release yourselves from any goliaths that come your way to impede your sight. Look over the horizon and see victory is at hand. Go forth with love, mercy, and kindness, for the new garments of humility doors will open an opportunity for newness the Lord is releasing for great things! Amen in Jesus name.

Gather the Stones:

In this hour, with so much greed and manipulation, you must protect your assets from being ruined by those who will steal and circumvent the truth to conceal their true intentions of harboring things and possessions for themselves.

So many people in all phases of life suffer at the hands of these malicious raiders. You must be careful not to fall prey to someone who says they care about you but take advantage of you; because of this action, vetting is imperative to your life and legacy. These types of spirits and people are in control and have all the power and will do whatever they can to make sure they finish on top, and whatever or whomever they must sacrifice to do this, and they are willing to do so without hesitation. Jesus spoke this parable about the tenants:

Luke 20:9-18 (NIV)
> He went to tell the people this parable:
> "A man planted a vineyard, rented it to some farmers and went away for a long time. At harvest time he sent a servant to the tenants so they would give him some of the fruit of the vineyard. But the tenants beat him and sent him away empty-handed. He sent another servant, but that one also they beat and treated shamefully and sent away empty- handed. He sent still a third, and they wounded him and threw him out. "Then the owner of the vineyard said, "what shall I do? I will send my son, whom I love; perhaps they will respect him.'
>
> But when the tenants saw him, they talked the matter over. "This is the heir,' they said let's kill him, and

28

the inheritance will be ours. So, they threw him out the vineyard and killed him.

"What then will the owner of the vineyard do to them? He will come and kill those tenants and give the vineyards to others.
When the people heard this, they said, "God forbid!"

Jesus looked directly at them and asked,
"Then what is the meaning of that which is written:
"The stone the builders rejected has become the cornerstone?

Everyone who falls on that stone will be broken to pieces; anyone on whom it falls will be crushed."

JUNTA:

A military or political group holding power after a revolution.

Boycott:

To unite, agreeing not to do business or associate with another nation for the purpose of punishment or coercion.

Coup:

> A sudden and decisive action in politics, especially one forcing change in government.

Cartel:

> A group of business (legal or illegal) that agree to work together.

Sanction:

> Action by several nations toward another, such as a blockade or economic restrictions, intended to force it to obey international law.

Due to the identification from the information listed in this section, these things can equate to everyday problems.

Matthew 24:6-7 (KJV)

> *Jesus told His disciples, "And ye shall hear of wars and rumors of wars: see that ye be not troubled: for all these things must come to pass, but the end is not yet. For nation shall rise against nation, and kingdom against kingdom: and there shall be famines, and pestilences, and earthquakes,*

30

DR. FREDRICK J. HARRIS

in divers' places."

II Timothy 1-5,7 (KJV)

> *Paul, writing to Timothy, told him, "This know also, that in the last days perilous times shall come. For men shall be lovers of their own selves, covetous, boasters, proud, blasphemers, disobedient to parents, unthankful, unholy. Without natural affection, trucebreakers, false accusers, incontinent, fierce, despisers of those that are good, traitors, heady minded, lovers of pleasures more than lovers of God; Having a form of godliness but denying the true power thereof; from such turn away. Ever learning, and never able to come to the knowledge of the truth."*

We are now experiencing many of these spiritual and natural disasters that Jesus Christ and the Apostle Paul said would occur in the last days. I will continue to do my part as an Apostle and Teacher of the Lord's word for His people. My prayer is that many will come into the right knowledge of God. Live for Him according to the word of God without shame and rebellion.

Overcoming Everyday Problems:

1. You must allow the spirit of God to feed your thought process. (II Corinthians 10:5) (Ephesians 5:18) (Matthew 4:4)

2. You must have a strong consciousness of your kingdom purpose. (Exodus 9:15-16) (Jeremiah 1:5) (Acts 17:26)

3. You must anchor your faith with the Hope of Glory. (Acts 20:32) (Hebrews 6:19-20) (Job 13:15)

4. You must discover the gift of helping others. (Hebrews 13:16) (John 3:11) (Matthew 6:24)

Work through these principles using God's wisdom, and you will not become so entangled and influence by the outside noise of those that do not have a desire to submit to the hand of God. (I Peter 5:6-7)

JUST TELL THE TRUTH

Nobody is above the LAW (Learn to Acknowledge Wisdom)
Why break the LAW to get what you cannot afford?

John 8:31-32 (NLT)
> *Jesus, said to the people who believe in him, "You are truly my disciples if you remain faithful to my teachings. And you will know the truth, and the truth will set you free."*

We are witnessing before our eyes disrespect of establishments and institutions in our country that support our way of life. The constant bombardment of lies and accusations of corruption have now bubbled up to the surface and spread like gangrene into the mainstream of public view.

This spirit is now moving about the country and the political influences without accountability, called tribalism.

Tribalism:
1. The state or fact of being organized in a tribe or tribes.
2. The behavior and attitudes that stem from strong loyalty to one's own tribe or social group.
3. Tribal consciousness and loyalty: especially exaltation of the tribe above other groups.

We see this as a society that has become motivated by cultural tribalism, as seen across every social media platforms and news outlets without apprehension. This behavior is a goliath of today because of big money interests and the select group that imposes control through all avenues of access to bring such corruption to people with lies and propaganda.

This spirit of tribalism is enhanced in the church circles of influence with evangelicals, whose money and resources are utilized to embolden the people elected to better the group.

Jesus warned us: Mark 8:14-21 (NIV)

The disciples had forgotten to bring bread, except for one loaf they had with them in the boat. "Be careful," Jesus warned them. "Watch out for the yeast of the Pharisees and that of Herod."

They discussed this with one another and said, "It is because we have no bread."

Aware of their discussion, Jesus asked them: "Why are you talking about having no bread? Do you still not see or understand? Are your hearts hardened?

Do you have eyes but fail to see, and ears but fail to hear? And don't you remember? When I broke the five loaves for the five thousand, how many basketfuls of pieces did you pick up?" "Twelve," they replied. "And when I broke the seven loaves for the four thousand, how man basketfuls of pieces did you pick up?" They answered, "seven." He said to them, "Do you still not understand?"

It is essential to tell the truth and do what is right. Never allow yourselves to

35

be placed in a position where you must compromise your integrity. There are many people in leadership positions that they cannot tell the truth about anything.

Telling lies is a permanent lifestyle for them. These people see themselves as above the law and are untouchable. Most people will not admit that there are problems in our society because it does not directly affect them, however, in the generations to come and the laws that are being put in place soon. Your children and grandchildren will indeed feel those laws because of the enormity of the events taking place.

I believe we have been receiving warning after warning, but the current generation does not want to accept the prophetic advice from the men and women of God assigned to be a voice in this hour.

Amos 3:6-7 (NLT)
When the ram's horn blows a warning, shouldn't the people be alarmed?
Does disaster come to a city unless the Lord has planned it?

Indeed, the Sovereign Lord never does anything until He reveals his plans to his servants, the prophets.

The audacious things that we are experiencing today are all a part of the plan of God. Stay in the place of observation and look for the facts of truth, not the sarcasm of lies.

Capitulate:

Cease to resist an opportunity or an unwelcome demand; surrender.

1. To surrender under specified conditions.
2. To give up all resistance; acquiesce
3. To accept military defeat
4. To accept something or agree to do something unwillingly.
5. To capitulate is to surrender or give up all demands.

The Military Victories of David:

I Chronicles 18:1-2 (NLT)

After David defeated and subdued the Philistines by conquering Gath and its surrounding towns. David also conquered the land of Moab, and the Moabites who were spared became David's subjects and paid him tribute money.

Money, power, and respect are several motivations that will cause people to capitulate for reasons beyond their standard control. You must be able to identify when the presence of this spirit to takeover is in your atmosphere.

As an educator, I work closely with children of various ages in the school sector. I have noticed the bullying spirit continues to grow and immerse itself in people's lives as a goliath. There must be strict accountability and programs that are going to eradicate this behavior. Bullying has become a stronghold to suppress people and families on many levels. There is no need to lie when questions are asked: "Just tell the truth?"

Truth can be brutal if one has never been held accountable or held responsible for lying. Once a liar is placed into a position of power, some bully others; believing bullying is the only avenue to remain in an authority position. This behavior is learned over years of unchecked traits and mannerisms. Tribalism is everywhere in our society, including churches.

The evangelicals are in silent support of this hostile takeover because it appears targeted towards a lower class of people and uneducated individuals who have dealt with frustrations and hostility their entire life.

There are demons and devils that have been in the shadows for years that are starting to emerge and spread these false lies that conjure up strife. People now are vacuumed into the portals of rage and anger. This has led to a generation of greed and selfishness. Their only concern is to get more wealth by any means necessary.

What a shame to bear witness to such blindness and watch people fall prey to deception and spiritual hypnosis. They are lulled into dark and dry places that bear no fruit for their lives.

Breaking of the covenant through a divorce:

Malachi 2:10 (NIV)
>Do we not all have one Father? Did not one God create us? Why do we profane the covenant of our ancestors by being unfaithful to one another?

Divorce:

1. The legal dissolution of a marriage by a court or other competent body.
2. Legally dissolve one's marriage with (someone).

3. Separate or dissolve (something) from something else.
4. Separation, severance, the divorce of the secular and the spiritual.

A judicial declaration dissolving a marriage in whole or in part, especially one that releases the marriage partners from all matrimonial obligations. Compare judicial separation, any formal separation of husband and wife.

Blame:
Assign responsibility for a fault or wrong.
An expression of disapproval or reproach: censure or saying nothing.
1. Deserving censure or disapproval; at fault: an

investigation to determine who
was to blame for the leak.

2. Being the cause or source of something.

We covered many points explaining in detail for those who need an in-depth understanding of how telling the truth is beneficial. However, many struggles are released because some people do not have the discipline for truths. We as a people must remain discipline because the truth is a powerful element for us to possess. Through this process, requirements there are to help facilitate the truth to stay intact. Facts are essential to enable people's accountability for their words and actions.

Proverbs 12:12-17 (NLT)
> *Thieves are jealous of each other's loot, but the godly are well rooted and bear their own fruit.*
>
> *The wicked are trapped by their own words, but the godly escape such trouble.*
>
> *Wise words bring many benefits, and hard work brings rewards. Fools think their own way is right, but the wise listen to others.*
> *A fool is quick-tempered, but a wise person stays calm when insulted.*

An honest witness tells the truth: a false witness tells lies.

As we close this chapter, be cognizant that telling the truth is very important. This behavior needs to be consistent and relevant to help God's people not only in the church but in our government at all levels.

Accountability is the key, and prayers are the foundations of hope in having a solidified structure to model after. By leading of the spirit of GOD, morality must come back to all the institutions of our infrastructure and the moral fabric of our churches. The spirit of unity is needed today in our complex and complicated society that is the driving force behind our communications. Telling the truth is not a bad thing; it is necessary for accountability and enables us to be more transparent with daily life. Tell the truth, and that is the way it is supposed to be.

5

REVOLUTIONS

The Impact of Dark Forces

Revolution:
1. A forcible overthrow of a government or social order in favor of a new system.
2. The American Revolution
3. (in Marxism) the class struggle, which is expected to

lead to political change and the triumph of communism.

4. An instance of revolving.

The overthrow or repudiation of a regime or political system by the governed. (*Derived from the* Marxist Theory) the violent and historically necessary transition from one system of production in society to the next, as from feudalism.

A body's progressive motion around an axis so that any line of the body parallel to the axis returns to its initial position while remaining parallel to the axis in transit and usually at a constant distance from it.

Ephesians 6:12-17 (NIV)

For struggle is not against flesh and blood, but against the rulers, against the authorities, against the powers of this dark world, and the spiritual forces of evil in the heavenly realms. Therefore, put on the full armor of God so that when the day of evil comes, you may be able to stand your ground, and you have done everything to stand. Stand firm then, with the belt of truth buckled around your waist, with the breastplate of righteousness in place, and your feet fitted with the readiness that comes from the gospel of peace. In addition to all this, take up the shield of faith, with which you can extinguish all the flaming arrows of the evil one. Take the helmet of salvation and the sword of the Spirit, which is the word of God.

The Word of God is (ARMOR)!

A- Activation, God will activate your faith. (Hebrews 11:1)

R- Restoration, God will completely restore everything. (I Samuel 30:8)

M- Manifestation, God will manifest miracles for you. (Luke 18:42-43)

O- Occupation, God will allow us to possess the land. (Numbers 14:8)

R- Reputation, God will protect His words over you. (I Peter 2:9-10)

ARMOR:

The metal coverings formerly worn by soldiers or warriors to protect the body in battle.

Provide (someone) with emotional, social, or other defenses.

A tough, protective covering, such as the bony scales, covering certain animals or the metallic plates on tanks and warships.

A safeguard or protection: faith, the missionary's armor.

There are certain things that have their place in this society. But here is the thing, they cannot hold us back from what God is going to do for us because He has made us powerful. When power is released during critical times, and you refuse to be truthful. Revolutions come in waves and are activated at pivotal times of crisis. I always believe that we must learn history from the past to understand why some things happen in our lives.

History:
(1777) (North Carolina)

The war between the colonies and England at first centered in the north. Massachusetts had the target of Parliament's efforts to "punish" the rebellious states. Therefore, much of the fighting took place in the Boston area. North Carolina was free of English troops, and the state seemed to have gained its goal of independence.

46

The War of 1812

The War of 1812 had an accidental beginning and an accidental ending. It began as the result of a war between England and France. These two countries were fighting at sea and often stopped American ships. When these foreign sailors boarded American ships, they would search for men from their lands and take these men from the vessel. The act of seizing persons from aboard a boat in this manner was called impressment. There were two reasons why Americans objected to this procedure. First, no country had (or has) the right to stop a ship from another country that is neutral in a war. Second, many Americans were mistakenly taken from these ships.

America protested these actions to both England and France. France stopped impressing sailors, but England continued the practice. The United States then tried to restrict trade with England, but this trade restriction hurt America more than England. Finally, President James Madison decided he would have to declare war on England. He did not know that England had agreed to stop impressing American sailors because communication from England took nearly two months. Poor communication allowed the war to start.

Nicaragua:

Nicaragua has a long history of unrest and civil disturbances. For 42 years, the country was ruled by members of the Somoza family - a father and two sons. The last son to rule, Anastasio, was very corrupt and lined his own pockets with money at his people's expense. A violent earthquake in 1972 destroyed much of Managua, the capital city. It killed more than 10,000 people and left almost 200,000 homeless. Much of the aid sent from other nations to help the earthquake victims ended up in Somoza's bank account.

These are just a few examples of the ruthlessness that unfolds amid revolutions. A calamity of every kind embeds itself deep in so many people's psyche because of the devastation that has taken place in their lives. Corruption is only one component of the schemes by these dark forces that have infiltrated our society.

The word of God gives us a clear perspective of what we are supposed to do when this spirit approaches. The problem is many people, including believers, do not want to confront such an adversary. Instead, they would act as though nothing is wrong and go on throughout life as if they are not being affected by dark forces. Jesus gave us plenty of reminders concerning this level of warfare. The question is, will anyone suit up to take on the threat of darkness that travels throughout the land, causing mayhem and chaos in the wake of destruction and deception?

Mark 7:6-15 (NIV)

> He replied, "Isaiah was right when he prophesied about you hypocrites; as it is written:
>
> "These people honor me with their lips, but their hearts are far from me. They worship me in vain; their teachings are merely human rules.' You have let go of the commands of God and are holding on to human traditions.
>
> "And he continued, "You have a fine way of setting aside the commands of God in order to observe your own traditions! For Moses said, 'Honor your father and mother, and, 'Anyone who curses their father or mother is to be put to death. But you say that if anyone declares that what might have been used to help their father or mother is Coban (that is, devoted to God) – then you no longer let them do anything for their father or mother. Thus, you nullify the word of·God by your tradition that you have handed down. And you do many things like that."
>
> Again, Jesus called the crowd to him and said, "Listen to me, everyone, and understand this. Nothing outside a person can defile them by going into them. Rather, it is what comes out of a person that defiles them."

History:

A chronological record of significant events (such as those affecting a

nation or institution) often explains their causes.

1. The study of past events particularly in human affairs.

2. The whole series of events connected with someone or something.

3. A continuous, typically chronological, record of important or public events or of a trend or institution.

As it pertains to the impact of dark forces, we must understand the history of things as they transpire. Often, we are emotionally moved by public events, and they can impact whether good or bad. Because of this, you must know how to weather the storm when it appears.

Through this process, wisdom is needed because there will be people who will experience catastrophic situations. They will need much aftercare to be restored to a place of wholeness. I have seen many circumstances that people go through and have no idea how to recover. Many remain captive through strongholds of drugs, alcohol, sex, anger, anxiety, suicide ideations, and many more destructive outlets because they entrapped to no end.

There must be solutions to the evil age we are experiencing, and the answer is Jesus.

John 10:11-18 (NIV)

"I am the good shepherd. The good shepherd lays down his life for the sheep. The hired hand is not the shepherd and does not own the sheep. So, when he sees the wolf coming, he abandons the sheep and runs away. Then the wolf attacks the flock and scatters it. The man runs away because he is a hired hand and cares nothing for the sheep.

"I am the good shepherd; I know my sheep and my sheep know me- just as the Father knows me and I know the Father – and I lay down my life for the sheep. I have other sheep that are not of this sheep pen. I must bring them also. They too will listen to my voice, and there shall be one flock and one shepherd. The reason my Father loves me is that I lay down my life – only to take it up again. No one takes it from me, but I lay it down of my own accord. I have authority to lay it down and authority to take it up again. This command I received from my Father."

After Care Is Needed:

1. Prayer for deliverance from demons.
    Matthew 8:28 - 34

2. Be sanctified by oil - Psalm 23:1 - 6

3. Fasting is necessary - Matthew 6:16 - 18

4. Consistent accountability over time.
   Romans 13:1 - 3

5. Follow the instructions to stay clean.
   John 13:6 - 17

6. Accept your assignment - Philippians 1:6

Conclusion:

Revolutions happen as something taken of significance to people and society at large. In most cases, these significant events have great consequences to all parties involved; therefore, a change must occur. Whenever the turmoil starts to take shape, you must have a strong support team that can assist with the aftermath of a revolution.

The same concept is displayed in the spiritual atmosphere because demonic forces and influences are real. They attach themselves to people and society to enhance the agenda of the kingdom of darkness. The satanic attachments and the illusions that accompany these spirits have embedded their roots in hidden places and cause great peril in many lives.

DR. FREDRICK J. HARRIS

Our focus needs to be laser sharp to pierce the principalities and the warfare surrounding it to block access from God's people in a powerful way. Utilize your wisdom and knowledge to make life better for those you love and respect and see the manifestation of miracles release to impact a generation into the marvelous light for the glory of God. I Peter 2:9 - 10

AVENGER'S INITIATIVE

The avenger's initiative compromises a team with unique abilities that enable the team to achieve its mission. They are in place to help those who are less fortunate and are not able to defend themselves. With this initiative, some defenses are positioned to ward off an onslaught of violent activity that may present itself amongst the people.

Initiative:

    1. The ability to assess and initiate
        things independently.

2. The power or opportunity to act or take charge before others do.

3. An act or strategy intended to resolve a difficulty or improve a situation; a fresh approach to something.

4. Especially in some US states and Switzerland the right of citizens outside the legislature to originate legislation.

5. An introductory act or step; leading action: to take the initiative in making friends.

Avenge:
1. Inflict harm in return for (an injury or wrong done to oneself or another).

2. Inflict harm on behalf of

(oneself or someone else
previously wronged or
charmed).

3. Revenge both to imply to
inflict pain or harm in return
for pain or harm inflicted on
oneself or those persons or
causes to which one feels
loyalty.

Ezekiel 25:17 (NIV)
*I will carry out great vengeance on them and punish
them in my wrath. Then they will know that I am
the Lord, when I take vengeance on them."*

I am reminded of the scripture James 1:19-21 (NIV):
*My dear brothers and sisters, take note of this:
Everyone should be quick to listen, slow to speak
and slow to become angry, because human anger
does not produce the righteousness that God desires.
Therefore, get rid of all moral filth and the evil that is
so prevalent and humbly accept the word planted in
you, which can save you.*

This passage of scriptures always helps me when I
am feeling overwhelmed by circumstances beyond my

control. It gives me great comfort because I am just like many other people who minister the gospel of Jesus. I take what I do seriously, and there are times I pray that many people who do not, would do the same thing. However, that is not the case. Often some people look at the word of God jokingly and interpret the scriptures sarcastically. I have learned some important principles about people, territorial spirits, manipulated illusions, and wicked principalities.

Principles to live by:

Hebrews 12:14-15 (NIV)
Make every effort to live in peace with everyone and to be holy; without holiness no one will see the Lord. See to it that no one falls short of the grace of God and that no bitter root grows up to cause trouble and defile many.

    A. Calm spirit of silence.
    B. Educate yourself with discipline.
    C. Cancel out all distractions.
    D. Have faith to overcome obstacles.
    E. Remain patient in all situations.
    F. Never carry a judgmental mindset
    G. Become a good giver.
    H. Be willing to go the extra mile.
    I. Never let deception drain you of victory.
    J. Rise to occasion
    K. Set and maintain your goals.
    L. Plan to prosper in all things.

M. Read to enhance your thoughts.

N. Meditate on the good and learn from the bad

O. Discern the law of attraction.

P. Take heed to the law of entanglement.

Q. Respect your values.

R. Protect your peace.

S. Construct your altar.

T. Develop a good posture of faith.

U. Understand your legacy for generations to come.

V. Root out any darkness that is trying to blind you.

W. Seek clarity from God.

X. Worship with a true spirit of repentance

Y. Thank God for provisions often.

Z. Do it all over again - consistency is the key.

If you can stabilize your faith and wisdom from this perspective. You can become so confident and vital that you will genuinely operate as an Avenger of faith, power, restoration, dreams, obedience, grace, love, and mercy. God can bring us into all understanding and truth. The problem is that too many people carry and form godliness and rely on the spirit of ideology and ignorance to keep them ensnared, and this creates a real crisis and releases chaos in cities and communities across America.

It is an absolute motricity that has overtaken this country and its people. The Apathy controlling the accountability in this hour is now not heard. Many are trying desperately to make a change in their sphere of influence while using the available resources to generate interest from an audience who undoubtedly are not desiring to hear God.

There must be proper alignment and focused on penetrating these dark forces, and we need Avengers to do so. The Avengers will take us into a spirit of gratitude with unfailing provisions from the Highest. This is an hour of a mass spiritual overhaul.

The world has infected its poison amongst the Lord's people for too long, and they are doing things with no checks and balances system. Every day, more and more demonized activities are showing themselves boldly in front of the television screens, movies, social media outlets, and videos. It is going to take a complete disaster for people to come back to the knowing of God and a true reverence for His presence.

As I look from this place of observation and influence, I have begun to master my frustrations and not allow others' inability to respond to God when He calls to interfere with my relationship and purpose to do His will. When I was much younger in my ministry development, I could only see things from a singular perspective. But through trials and tribulations, I noticed how inept many people have become. I wanted to impact bringing God glory, and I yielded myself to His spirit for teaching and training. Because I realized I must function in several areas of focus at different times. Therefore, I signed up for the Avenger Initiative. We are in a war, and as these battles continue to rage on, there is a severe famine taking place for the lack of faith and understanding, and people do not seem to care.

Hosea 4:4-7 (NLT)
> *"Don't point your finger at someone else and try to pass the blame!*
> *My complaint, you priests, is with you. So, you will stumble in the broad daylight, and your false prophets will fall with you in the night. And I will destroy Israel, your mother.*
>
> *My people are being destroyed because they don't know me. Since you priests refuse to know me, I refuse to recognize you as my priests.*
>
> *Since you have forgotten the laws of your God, I will forget to bless your children. The more priests there are, the more they sin against me. They have exchanged the glory of God for the shame of idols.*

Nahum 2:8-10 (NLT)
> *Nineveh is like a leaking water reservoir! The people are slipping away. "Stop, stop!" someone shouts, but no one even looks back.*

Loot the silver! Plunder the gold! There's no end to Nineveh's treasures-its vast wealth. Soon the city is plundered, empty, and ruined. Hearts melt and knees shake. The people stand aghast, their faces pale and trembling.

Nahum 3:11-12 (NLT)

And you, Nineveh, will also stagger like a drunkard. You will hide for fear of the attacking enemy. All your fortresses will fall. They will be devoured like the ripe figs that fall into the mouths of those who shake the trees.

We live in a time where you see so much peril and destruction. And it is time to take a stand against all the wickedness. We can bear witness to the rotting decay in our neighborhoods, school systems, job markets, political election systems, and so much more. As you witness these experiences, what do you think should be done to right the wrongs?

The next generation must be protected from all the mayhem we are affected by daily. There are several instances of the drama and the consequences for what is portrayed. As an avenger, I am fixated on stepping up to do my part. What is frustrating to watch is the cynical approach by the more seasoned mature population. The Bible gave us multiple examples where the very elect was deceived. This is not only in the church, but you see it everywhere, and this runaway spirit must be crush to a pulp.

61

You may be saying to yourself, how do we get rid of this spirit?

1. Prayer- changes everything
2. Evangelize- this can be a recruiting mechanism for souls to be saved.
3. Inspire- encouraging those around you has an impact.
4. Let go- if there is no change, you must let go.
5. Strategy- there must be a plan for success.
6. Protect- cover your investments by the Blood of Christ.
7. Boldness- stay on guard.
8. Set the example- it is hard, but it must be done.
9. Teach- become a mentor to a lost generation.

In the essence of understanding the Avenger Initiative, you must be willing to lead from the front and take the fight to the enemy. There is no time to relax and be nonchalant. It is a strong and prideful principality that must be conquered at all costs. We in the last and evil days, and we must fight with a relentless attitude and determination.

The fact is the more we engage the enemy in his territory; we will not have to fight him on ours. Too many people are giving up ground to an enemy and losing the battle because they have no stamina or strength to continue the good fight of faith for Christ Jesus.

PROPHETIC DEGREE:

God is raising prophetic arrows that are ready to engage in war. This remnant is locked and loaded with an arsenal that will penetrate deep into the enemy's camp and take back the people's possessions. In this hour, the shofar has sounded, the trumpets are blaring, and the walls are ready to tumble. So, people of God, release yourself for victory and become an avenger of movement for the greater upon us possess a large land flowing with milk and honey. Increase your weapons from your stockpile of faith and allow God Almighty to take you deeper and deeper in the battle of time.

You are battle-tested and built to last soldiers of God. Tighten your boots and put on your uniform. You have enlisted into the army of God, and you will complete your mission. God awaits you to arise and conqueror for your treasures in your hand. Now, use your weaponry of prayer and sanctification to release from on high, God is leading you into victory to receive your crown. In Jesus name, amen.

Conclusion:

The Avengers Initiative is an anchor of faith for firm believers to collectively labor with other believers to settle the score. The weapons in your armory are ready to be activated for the supreme task at hand.

God requires us to dominate and take back what is rightfully ours. Be a fighter, be a warrior, and be an Avenger.

Psalm 28:4-5 (NIV)
Repay them for their deeds and for their evil work; repay them for what their hands have done and bring back on them what they deserve. Because they have no regard for the deeds of the Lord and what His hands have done, He will tear them down and never build them up again.

Isaiah 48:4-5 (NLT)
For I know how stubborn and obstinate you are. Your necks are as unbending as iron. Your heads are as hard as bronze. That is why I told you what would happen; I told you beforehand what I was going to do. Then you could never say, 'My idols did it.

Amos 8:11-12 (NLT)
"The time is surely coming," says the Sovereign Lord, "When I will send a famine on the land-not a famine of bread or water but of hearing the words of the Lord.

People will stagger from sea to sea and wander from border to border searching for the word of the Lord, but they will not find it.

WEAPONS of MASS DESTRUCTION

In March 2003, American Servicemembers were called upon to respond to the global war on terrorism. In this unprecedented move by the U.S. Government and Congress, a joint public session of the congress held to discuss the weapon capability possessed by Saddam Hussein, who was President of Iraq.

Public briefings were presented to the American public, the significance of authorizing Iraq's invasion and occupation to remove Saddam Hussein from power. Upon completing this mission, Soldiers would be responsible for establishing sustain and stability in a war-torn country. Throughout this ordeal, the mandate was to find and destroy all weapons of mass destruction. US Troops have been serving in Iraq for well over 15 years; no weapons were discovered.

Death to an Idol and Nation:

I Chronicles 10:1-7 (NIV)

Now the Philistines fought against Israel; the Israelites fled before them, and many fell dead on Mount Gilboa. The Philistines were in hot pursuit of Saul and his sons, and they killed his sons Jonathan, Abinadad and Malki-Shua. The fighting grew fierce around Saul, and when the archers overtook him, they wounded him.

Saul said to his armor-bearer, "Draw your sword and run me through, or these uncircumcised fellows will come and abuse me."

But his armor-bearer was terrified and would not do it; so, Saul took his own sword and fell on it. When the armor-bearer saw that Saul was dead, he too fell on his sword and died. So, Saul and his three sons died, and all his house died together.

When all the Israelites in the valley saw that the army had fled and that Saul and his sons had died, they abandoned their towns and fled. And the Philistines came and occupied them.

How does this story correlate to weapons of mass destruction? When there are rogue leaders in powerful positions, they will abuse this authority for their benefit because of greed.

When you investigate our modern history of time, we are in a period of complete disillusion because we have the President of the United States who operates with an impulse spirit. We do not know the actual ramifications of his erratic behavior that has already caused so many people to experience calamity from his actions.

It is happening all over the world and especially in our country. The American people are expecting our elected officials to hold the administration responsible for their mismanagement of affairs. Many politicians have been entirely silent to pledge allegiance to lousy behavior instead of good moral conduct and transparency.

<u>Pragmatism:</u>

Pragmatism as a philosophical tradition began in the United States around 1870. Pragmatism rejects the idea that the function of thought is to describe, represent, or mirror reality. Instead, pragmatists consider thought an instrument or tool for prediction, problem solving and action.

Pragmatism:
1. A pragmatic attitude or policy.

2. An approach that assesses the truth
3. of meaning of theories or beliefs in
    terms of the success of their
    practical application.

Everything is achievable through technology, even the development of weapons that destroy people's future. Not only natural weapons but spiritual weapons also. It is very imperative to be in tune with your weapons in the proper season of your life. Teaching and mentoring are essential tools that will help fight off these dangerous arrows streaming towards you.

2 Corinthians 10:3-5 (NIV)
> *For though we live in the world, we do not wage war as the world does. The weapons we fight with are not the weapons of the world. On the contrary, they have divine power to demolish strongholds. We demolish arguments and every pretension that sets itself up against the knowledge of God, and we take captive every thought to make it obedient to Christ.*

WEAPON:

A weapon, arm or armament is any device that can be used with intent to inflict damage or harm.

Weapons are used to increase the efficacy and efficiency of activities such as hunting, crime, law enforcement, self-defense, and warfare. In broader context, weapons may be construed to include anything used to gain a tactical, strategic, material, or mental advantage over an adversary or enemy target.

This information is used in several areas of influence to include the church and the political spheres, that enable evil-minded individuals to do heinous things to others with any regard to life or safety. Investigate society's apparatus and the many challenges that people face; it appears all hope is lost.

Tours of Duty in Foreign Territory:

As I reflect on my two deployments to Iraq and one time to Afghanistan, I recall seeing agony in the citizens' faces. The people were under extreme oppression for decades, with ruthless dictators leading both countries into a pit without compassion or empathy.

There are hundreds of nations worldwide under the curse of tyranny, and famines have dominated the regions with no end in sight. This is not what God intended for the earth to look like from man's abuse and ideology. As I continued my year-long deployments, I would find myself trying to remain focused on the mission and encourage my soldiers at every opportunity. The task was not easy to maintain. I also needed encouragement because of personal issues I was facing in my own life. Somehow, God would always give me the inner strength to keep going.

Fighting the war on terrorism has its extreme consequences. Your life is still in danger, and you must rely on your relationship with God and your training for specific circumstances. I noticed a significant number of soldiers and civilians showing up to the chapel for services every chance they got. It was a welcomed opportunity but very challenging because many people did not have a strong faith or a closeness with God.

Whenever there was an encounter with faith versus flesh, the power of God must come in and establish victory for these people's lives. It was a matter of them demonstrating a willingness to trust God in times of uncertainty. As a leader in the faith, I was responsible for helping these soldiers develop their connection with God, and I wanted to make sure the spirit of God led me.

The Gathering of Men:

Numbers 11:16-17(KJV)
> *And the Lord said unto Moses, gather unto me seventy men of the elders of Israel, whom thou*

knowest to be the elders of the people, and officers over them; and bring them unto the tabernacle of the congregation, that they may stand there with thee.

And I will come down and talk with thee there: and I will take of the spirit which is upon thee and will put it upon them; and they shall bear the burden of the people with thee, that thou bear it not thyself alone.

We must never do things on our own and feel there is no help in sight for us. God has never called anyone to all the work on their own, and He does not like when crooked men take advantage of good people for their gain. This spirit is called selfish behavior, and God will deal with this spirit accordingly over time.

Satan knows if your eyes opened to the truth of the gospel of Christ, you will be changed into the image of Christ. This truth of transformation is the purpose for beholding the light of the Gospel. You do not have to carry yourself like a weapon of mass destruction and be treated as a puppet where you are repeatedly ignored and disrespected.

Hebrews 4:12-13 (NKJV)
For the word of God is quick, and powerful, and sharper than any two-edged sword, piercing even to the dividing asunder of soul and spirit, and of the joints and marrow, and is a discerner of the thoughts

and intents of the heart.

Neither is there any creature that is not manifest in his sight: but all things are naked and opened unto the eyes of him with whom we must do.

Conclusion:

God desires for us to be awakened in truth and not ignorance. We have enough nonsense unfolding each day in society. There is a silent spirit that has attached itself to people and their lives to keep them suppressed and depressed to the point where they feel that no success will ever come.

Put yourself in a position for increase and opportunity, and do not succumb to the snares that are often associated with negative results. Trust God in everything and build your relationship with HIM through love, faith, and hope. The greatest of these is love.

I Corinthians 13:13 (NIV)
And now these three remain: faith, hope and love. But the greatest of these is love.

SATAN IS A CREATURE

Have you ever asked yourself, what is the meaning of a creature? When a person refers to anything as a creature, our thoughts can only negatively view the statement.

However, God made it clear to us that He created every creature and every living thing according to:

Genesis 1:30 (NIV)
> And to all the beasts of the earth and all the birds in the sky and all the creatures that move along the ground- everything that has the breath of life in it-I give every green plant for food." And it was so.

Creature:

An animal, distinct from a human being

1. An animal or person

2. A fictional or imaginary being, typically a frightening one.

3. Anything living or existing

4. A person of specified kind, typically one viewed with pity, contempt, or desire.

5. A person or organization considered to be under the complete control of another.

<u>Satan</u>:

Satan, also known as the devil, is an entity in the Abrahamic religions that seduces humans into sin or falsehood. In Christianity and Islam, he is usually seen as either a fallen angel or a jinn, who used to possess great piety and beauty but rebelled against God, who nevertheless allows him temporary power over the fallen world and a host of demons. In Judaism, Satan is typically regarded as a metaphor for the yetzer hara, or "evil inclination," or as an agent subservient to God.

In Christianity, Satan is also known as the Devil and, although the Book of Genesis does not mention him, he is often identified as the serpent in the Garden of Eden. In the Middle Ages, Satan played a minimal role in Christian theology and was used as a comic relief figure in mystery plays. During the early modern period, Satan's significance greatly increased as beliefs such as demonic possession and witchcraft became more prevalent. During the Age of Enlightenment, belief in the existence of Satan became harshly criticized.

Nonetheless, belief in Satan has persisted, particularly in the Americas. In the Quran, Shaitan, also known as Iblis, is an entity made of fire who was cast out of Heaven because he refused to bow before the newly created Adam and incites humans to sin by infecting their minds with evil suggestions. Satan is known as evil; however, some groups have very different beliefs.

According to the Barna Group, many Christians do not believe that Satan or the devil exists. However, according to an AP - AOL news poll, up to 97% of evangelical Christians believe that angels exist. Contrary to the beliefs of many, Satan is not the opposite of God – anti-god. According to the Bible, Satan is a created being, having been created by God.

Job 1:6-12 (NIV)
> One day the angels came to present themselves before the Lord, and Satan also came with them. The Lord said to Satan, "where have you come from?"
>
> Satan answered the Lord, "From roaming throughout the earth, going back and forth on it."
>
> Then the Lord said to Satan, "Have you considered my servant Job? There is no one on earth like him; he is blameless and upright, a man who fears God and shuns evil."
>
> "Does Job fear God for nothing?" Satan replied. "Have you not put a hedge around him and his household and everything he has? You have blessed the work of his hands, so that his flocks and herds are spread throughout the land. But now stretch out your hand and strike everything he has, and he will surely curse you to your face."

The Lord said to Satan, "Very well, then, everything he has is in your power, but on the man, himself do not lay a finger. Then Satan went out from the presence of the Lord. God created Satan for a purpose, and this is why he is considered a creature. His assignment is to engage in warfare that causes chaos in people's lives according to God's permissive will. He cannot do anything of his own accord unless God allows it.

God does certain things that we cannot comprehend sometimes, but the most impressive thing is that He will bring us out of any trouble to rejoice and praise Him with understanding. When trials occur, we should never enhance the agenda of Satan without first asking God for wisdom.

Situations that many people face is generated out of the purposed time for the event to take place. So, never sit there and ask God why things are happening, and then you start complaining. There is a time factor that has activated, and you must know that the creature of Satan has entered your orbit to push you to greater blessings from God. God has ordered your steps.

Ecclesiastes 3:1 (NIV)
> There is a time for everything, and a season for every activity under the heavens.

Psalm 37:1-2 (NIV)
> Do not fret because of those who are evil or be envious of those who do wrong; for like the grass they will soon wither, like green plants they will soon die away.

Psalm 37:23 (NIV)

The Lord makes firm the steps of the one who delights in him; though they stumble, he will not fall, for the Lord upholds him with his hand.

I was young and now I am old, yet I have never seen the righteous forsaken or their children begging bread.

Satan makes attempts to eat anything he can concerning you. That is why you must attend training sessions on warfare from the enemy. You must remember he is a creature, and there is no substance on him that you cannot overcome. God has a plan, and He protects you from being thrown off course, even though sometimes it may not feel like it. The schemes and tactics there have to be protections in place to stand against Satan's attacks.

Protections from Satan:

1. Pray without ceasing.
2. Fight for your future.
3. Move-in silence.
4. Understand situational awareness.
5. Stay vigilant about your assignment.
6. Maintain a relentless approach to victory.
7. Keep your ear to the mouth of God.
8. Demonstrate patience during times of darkness.
9. Keep a song of worship in your spirit.
10. Know that God is able in all things.

We wrestle not against flesh and blood. Always ask God for His insight to wisdom to overcome the fiery darts of Satan. Remember, he is a creature, and God has an order of protection around you. Your fruit shall remain as long you are determined for a good outcome. The Lord is a keeper.

Philippians 1:6 (NLT)

And I am certain that God who began a good work within you, will continue His work until it is finally finished on the day when Christ Jesus returns.

ANGELS & DEMONS

This chapter will discuss the interactions of angels as well as demons. There is a war going on, and as believers, we must be prepared for battle. In 1 Chronicles 11, David is in his place of leadership over his armies. He has prepared his fighters well, and now they are allowed to display leadership skills and personal protection with the king. Because of this interaction, every God-given opportunity comes with God-given responsibility. Therefore, we must listen to the wisdom of our angels during times of battle. And be equipped to trounce every demon that will embolden itself against the plan God has for us.

Exodus 14:19-20 (NLT)

> Then the angel of God, who had been leading the people of Israel, moved to the rear of the camp. The pillar of cloud also moved from the front and stood behind them. The cloud settled between the Egyptian and Israelite camps. As darkness fell, the cloud turns to fire, lighting up the night. But the Egyptians and Israelites did not approach each other all night.

Matthew 4:1-4 (NLT)

> Then Jesus was led by the Spirit into the wilderness to be tempted there by the devil. For forty days and forty nights he fasted and became very hungry. During that time the devil came and said to him, "If you are the Son of God, tell these stones to become loaves of bread."

> But Jesus told him, "No! The Scriptures say, 'People do not live by bread alone, but by every word that comes from the mouth of God.'"

ANGELS:

Angels help people! Yes, God uses his faithful angels to help people today. God uses angels as he directs his servants in preaching the good news of the Kingdom of God.

An angel is a pure spirit created by God. The Old Testament theology included the belief in angels: the name applied to individual spiritual beings or intelligence of heavenly residence, employed by God as ministering spirits.

Angels are ministering spirits and do not have physical bodies like humans.

Angels bring the joy of miracles into your daily lives for encouragement, inspiration, and revelation.

DEMONS:

The Bible teaches and gives evidence that demons exist. The word of demons in Greek is daimon.

Demons are known as Satan's evil angels. A demon is a supernatural and often malevolent being prevalent in religion.

Demonology:
This is the systematic study of demons or beliefs about demons. It is the branch of theology relating to supernatural beings who are not gods. It deals both with benevolent beings with no circle of worshippers or limited a process below, are the rank of gods, and with malevolent being of all kinds.

Angels are here to bless you for the glory of God. One of the main issues that I have witnessed in ministry or the marketplace is people not taking the time to enjoy their relationships with angels that God has assigned to their lives. I have heard people say, "I am scared to speak with an angel." The angel offers advice, protection, wisdom, grace, understanding, guidance, favor, and many other benefits that come with this relationship.

However, it seems as though people would rather entertain and give more credence to demons rather than angels. I believe it comes from a lack of understanding and teachings in various capacities.

The (F.E.A.R) factor infiltrates the mind and gives off the stigma of false evidence appearing real. Fear is an actual demon for people to escape the devil's traps and because of the ability to transfer evil spirits. We must address them when recognized.

II Timothy 1:7 (NLT)
God has given us a spirit of fear and timidity, but power, love, and self-discipline.

You must maintain self-discipline today because the demons have become bolder in the daylight and not just at night. They practice witchcraft, sorcery, and divination in the open now without any accountability for their actions. You do not have to look far to see the demonic activity being release when the President of the United States is the biggest violator demonstrating no restraints in his behavior on social media. This is direct in your face demonized attitude towards the people of God and no reproach for his antics; but we do have angels that are on guard to protect the interest of the people today.   84

They show up in different forms and are imperative to our society and way of life today. If you watch the news and movies, the demonic forces have engaged in an all-out assault upon people who stand for truth. What is appalling is the notion of silence from the people in positions of power and influence who enable this behavior to affect everyday life for most people. The spirit of greed, fame, and lustful intentions has risen to an all-time high when pastors allow anything to stand in the pulpit and speak over people. Then, the spirit of divination has introduced occults and legions of followers in the witchcraft religion.

The church is growing, but the spirit of manipulation is overpowering and cause people to stay away from the church. We must engage the problem with solutions and have resources available to bring consistency to people's lives.

In Latin America, the Bible has become popular in several countries it is sold in markets and department stores. The Christianity movement has spread rapidly in prominent communities and countries across South America that Church leaders have moved into larger locations because of the vast growth to their congregations.

They have moved to the point of several weekly services, and with the abundance of members, the churches could only have worship services

85

once a month to fit the need of their congregants.

A church in Guatemala City, the capital of Guatemala, has more than 4,000 members and a large school. The Southern Baptist work among the Kekchi Indians has been quite successful. Believers have established several schools using the Biblical curriculum in Guatemala.

In Mexico, missionaries labored for years with little success. Today Bible-believing churches are springing up throughout Mexico. The total number of evangelical churches has risen to somewhere between 10,000 and 15,000.

North America:

Today in the United States and Canada, many people claim to be Believers. However, the United States and Canada have not experienced a growing Christian church such as other parts of the world. The humanist education system, media, and mind-set have trained North Americans to reason away much of the Bible and its teachings. Many have become complacent and have stopped seeking a spiritual awakening. Some Believers have lost their enthusiasm for God's Word and have stopped expecting Him to demonstrate His power in their lives and churches.

II Timothy 3:1-5 (NLT)

> *You should know this, Timothy that in the last day there will be very difficult times. For people will love only themselves and their money. They will be boastful and proud, scoffing at God, disobedient to their parents, and ungrateful. They will consider nothing sacred. They will be unloving and unforgiving; they will slander others and have no self-control. They will betray their friends, be reckless, be puffed up with pride, and love pleasure rather than God. They will act religious, but they will reject the power that could make them godly. Stay away from people like that!*

Apostle Paul discussed this wisdom to help Timothy stay focused on ministry and impact the church and community. I believe that the true essence of the community is vastly different from 30 years ago. Many neighborhoods have not gotten better but worse. The Shepard's hearts are missed in the communities and churches around this nation and the world.

There is a severe demonic attack on churches and communities today. There are churches on every corner, but do these leaders truly have the heart to shepherd God's people. Their focus must be on the people and not getting rich off the people. There must be relationships of love and mercy for people who have suffered for many years, especially at marauders' hands, who all they do is take from the weaker or lesser people. That is what I call "prophetic bullying" or a pulpit bully.

When the church's leadership functions in this manner, the devil will send attacks to separate the people and leadership from their assigned purpose. It is a divided wedge brought in by the enemy, which is the cause of many contentious and rebellious acts by spirits and people. By understanding the leadership roles, the church can triumph over any assaults from the enemy and help the people know when angels arrive on the scene, they come to be a blessing, not a curse.

Chasing after worldly possessions and things is not wise for men and women of God. They are supposed to act like angels and protectors of the Lord's people. Encouraging them and bringing them into a closer relationship with God. These are very trouble times, so do not waste your energy on fruitless and troubled people and places.

Our government is supposed to be a beacon of order and standards. Daily, when you look in your news feeds or at news stations, the government sets the bar real low for the unity of its people of this country. A sad display of demonic influences from multiple areas in our government, and it is a despicable presentation of moral conduct gone rogue. It is time for someone to stand against these wayward spirits releasing demons into our society and way of life.

Ecclesiastes 4:4-6 (NIV)
> *And I saw that all toil and all achievement spring from one person's envy of another. This too is meaningless, a chasing after the wind. Fools fold their hands and ruin themselves. Better one handful of tranquility than two handfuls with toil and chasing after the wind.*

Conclusion:

Angels are real, and they exist to help and protect. Demons are real because they come to disrupt and destroy. The purpose of learning sound doctrine is to know how to be strong as angels and defeat any demon that comes into your path. You have a direct assignment from God, and you must complete the mandate. So, move forward with power and revelation to utilize your strengths and abilities to bring forth great glory for the kingdom of God. Stay strong and do not give up. Keep other around you accountable as well and fight the good fight of faith. God loves His soldiers, and you are trained for the battle.

A VINDICTIVE SPIRIT

This chapter will demonstrate to you the ability to overcome a vindictive spirit. Evils spirits are always present among us, from this place of sensitivity where the fiery darts cannot consume you from social media platforms and news outlets showcasing these vengeful spirits without regard for people's feelings or state of being.

We have leadership in our churches today and in our government and communities with no compassion or empathy for people. And it is a far cry from what we were accustomed to years ago. There must be civility in all things and respect shown at all levels. But the sad part is we have leaders that feel and think they are above the law in the natural and in the spirit.

When a church and people change their values to match society's climate or current culture, they are no longer following the word of God, and they are following the lost at all cost.

VINDICTIVE:

Having or showing a strong or unreasoning desire for revenge.

1. Disposed to seek revenge. Vengeful
2. Intended for or involving revenge.
3. Intended to cause anguish or hurt; spiteful.
4. Showing malicious ill will and a desire to hurt, motivated by spite.

"A vindictive man will look for occasions for resentment."

The vindictive politics of the time may have pushed the nation over the abyss, but at least the cadres

were squeaky clean. It is childish
and hateful to manufacture petty,
vindictive cliques who seem to
thrive on aloofness and
exclusivity. According to English
by Oxford.

God is our Great Equalizer:

He is the equalizer because He oversees
everything. He knows what we need when we need it.
That is the most important thing, and it is necessary for
our development and growth.

Testimony:

After almost 20 years of ministry and serving 26 years
in the military, I am dedicated to serving, for I am a
servant. In these last few years, I have been
a wakened by the Holy Spirit to more and more
truths about the church's conditions, our society at
large, and the government overall.

I must say the Bible is right about all things inscribed
in it. We as a people must take God seriously at this
time of our lives. Pay attention to the life of Jesus
and all his sacrifices for us as humankind. He
paved the way for us to have a blessed family of
God, and we must not take this for granted. He gives

us instructions that will increase our lives and not run wild throughout the journey.

I am tired of seeing schemes and scams that are penetrating lives and wreaking havoc at every turn. That is why I ask God to strengthen me to become a great teacher of His word and lead people in wisdom and revelation for His glory. This generation is lukewarm that will not sacrifice anything or go the distance for the Kingdom of God.

My prayer is one day, this generation will come into the full acknowledgment of God and what He desires most, and it greater than anything they could fathom for themselves.

The enemy does not play or fight fair. But God has equipped us for victory on every side, no matter the challenge.

II Chronicles 7:14-15 (KJV)
> *If my people, which are called by my name, shall humble themselves, and pray, and seek my face, and turn from their wicked ways; then will I hear from heaven, and will forgive their sins, and will heal their land.*
>
> *Now mine eyes shall be open, and mine ears attent unto the prayer that is made in this place.*

Taking scripture at its word bring value to me

and all who adhere to the word of God. At one point in my life, I did not know where to turn or what to do. I would ask questions about the word of God, as I got older to understand it help to truly grow in my faith and trust God no what came my way.

Again, my prayer is for others to do the same and trust God. When your pastors and leaders are there for training and Bible study, please attend and take good notes. If you decide you do not want to do so, then do not waste your leader's time because you do not want to change!

Combat the Vicious Voices:

Deuteronomy 30:2 (KJV)
And shalt return unto the Lord thy God, and shalt obey his voice according to all that I command thee this day, thou and thy children, with all thine heart, and with all thy soul;

1. Know your prophetic language.
2. Have a strong position of faith.
3. Use all your weapons in your arsenal.
4. Stay committed for victory.
5. Find value in your failures.
6. Do all things with confidence.
7. Release your power.
8. Run your race with gladness.

There are toxic things taking place in the world. Because of all that is transpiring and the negativity is spreading profusely across the landscape, the spirit of revenge and hatred are dominating communities and neighborhoods. We must eradicate this behavior and remove it from society, our churches, and the government. We need a strategy to change our circumstances and look for the betterment of what we desire in life. If we do not start having solutions, then we continue to have an angry posture towards the origin of hostility.

The beginning starts with someone or something that has been planting seeds of discord for a long time until it becomes grown without accountability.

James 1:19-22 (NIV)

> My dear brothers and sisters, take note of this: Everyone should be quick to listen, slow to speak and slow to become angry, because human anger does not produce the righteousness that God desires. Therefore, get rid of all moral filth and the evil that is so prevalent and humbly can save you. Do not merely listen to the word, and so deceive yourselves. Do what it says.

Observation:

1. The action or process of observing something or someone carefully or in order to gain information.

2. The ability to notice things, especially significant details.
3. The taking of the altitude of the sun or another celestial body for navigational purposes.
4. A remark, statement, or comment based on something one has seen, heard, or noticed.

Observation:

Is the active acquisition of information from a primary source. In living beings, it employs the senses.

In science, it can also involve the recording of data via the use of instruments. The term may also refer to any data collected during the scientific activity.

I can only speak what I see from my prophetic sphere:

Prophetic Eye:

As God has dealt with me over the years, I can see the constant downturn of wisdom and respect. More and more people are on edge because they do not have a strong faith walk with God. In retrospect, the wisdom needed for today has shifted to the point where there is no accountability or consequences for leading people in the wrong way of life.

Calamity and disaster have washed ashore into people's foundation, and they look like sheep headed to the slaughter. People have gone so far as to mutilate their bodies and minds through tattoos and plastic surgery. Their health is deteriorating quickly due to a false narrative in expression to choose painstaking procedures over the Lord's teachings.

Revenge and vindictiveness are everywhere across the world. Very little compassion is displayed, and the (dogma) spirit has unleashed to promote an evil agenda in society. God told us through various books and chapters of the Bible that this would come.

Here it is, and we need protection on every side to defeat a strong enemy whose assignment is to sow chaos. The levels of unpreparedness of people are horrifying and depressing to witness. Something should be done to those spiritual leaders who influence money, resources, and national platforms

97

to galvanize people to follow God and not the world's corrupt systems.

It is time to stand for what is right and just for the people of the Lord. We must unify as one Army for the glory of God and continue to reach out in multiple ways to connect the heart of the children back to the Father in Heaven. So, men and women of God preach, teach, minister, pray, activate, train, develop, and implement strategies that will change people, nations, and the world. In Jesus' name!

Ezekiel 33:1-9 (NIV)
The word of the Lord came to me: "Son of man, speak to your people and say to them: 'When I bring the sword against a land, and the people of the land choose one of their men and make him their watchman, and he sees the sword coming against the land and blows the trumpet to warn the people, then if anyone hears the trumpet but does not heed the warning and the sword comes and take their life, their blood will be on their own head. Since they heard the trumpet but did not heed the warning, their blood will be on their own head. If they had heeded the warning, they would have saved themselves. But if the watchman sees the sword coming and does not blow the trumpet to warn the people and the sword comes and takes someone's life, that person's life will be taken because of their sin, but I will hold the watchman accountable for their blood.'

"Son of man, I have made you a watchman for the

people of Israel; so, hear the word I speak and give them warning from me. When I say to the wicked, 'You wicked person, you will surely die,' and you do not speak out to dissuade them from their ways, that wicked person will die for their sin, and I will hold you accountable for their blood. But if you do warn the wicked person to turn from their ways and they do not do so, they will die for their sin, though you yourself will be saved.

This scripture states what will happen if you do not take heed to what God is saying. I believe this is the period we are in now for this generation. All these must take shape in a society gone wrong, from police brutality to school shootings across the country. The hostility of violence is out of control, and our elected leaders do not see a problem because it does not affect them directly. The spirit of denial is loose in the atmosphere, and it must be annihilated.

Exodus 1:11-14 (NLT)

So, the Egyptians made the Israelites their slaves. They appointed brutal slave drivers over them, hoping to wear them down with crushing labor. They forced them to build cities of Pithom and Rameses as supply centers for the king. But the more the Egyptians oppressed them, the more the Israelites multiplied and spread, and the more alarmed the Egyptians became. So, the Egyptians worked the people of Israel without mercy. They made their lives bitter, forcing them to mix mortar and make bricks and do all the work in the fields. They were ruthless in all their demands.

The Report Is Out:

A description of something or information about it to someone: to be described by people as being or doing a thing although there is no real proof: to make a complaint to a person in authority.

A report is a collection of information about something or rumors or gossip that is being spread.

A document that presents information in an organized format for a specific audience and purpose. Although summaries of reports may be delivered orally, complete reports are almost always written documents.

1. Give a spoken or written account of something that one has observed, heard, done, or investigated.

2. Present oneself formally as having arrived at a place or as ready to do something.

3. Be responsible to (a superior or supervisor).

NOUN:

1. An account given of a matter, especially in the form of an official

document, after thorough investigation or consideration by an appointed person or body.

2. A piece of information that is unsupported by firm evidence and that the speaker feels may or may not be true.

3. A sudden loud noise of or like an explosion or gunfire.

4. An employee who is supervised by another employee.

Because we are in the most robust information age of our time, the reporting process happens quickly, and you must adjust when necessary because all the reporting agency is available. During the Old Testament period, information was disseminated over days, weeks, and even months. Many of the Prophets of Old talked with God and received His council and pass it along to the appointed officials on time. However, most of the scribes gave the information to messengers who had to travel long distances to transmit it.

Proverbs 22:17-23 (NIV)

Pay attention and turn your ear to the sayings of the wise; apply your heart to what I teach, for it is pleasing when you keep them in your heart and have all of them ready on your lips.

So, that your trust may be in the Lord, I teach you today, even you. Have I not written thirty sayings for you, sayings of counsel and knowledge, teaching you to be honest and to speak the truth, so that you bring back truthful reports to those you serve?

The question I would ask? Can we see this happening in the church and our society today? The vindictive spirit is consistently raging over and over, again and again. Strategies that become a combat force multiplier must be activated for such a time as this.

<u>Combat Force Multiplier</u>:

Combat:
Two-Way Communication

    A. Wisdom Is Your Advantage-
    B. Transparency Bring Deliverance-
    C. Defend Your Territory-
    D. Learn from Your Mistakes-
    E. Trust Your Inner Circle-
    F. Never Accept Poverty as Your Normal-
    G. Walk with Strength and Power-

H. Expect the Impossible Blessings-
I. Establish Strong Relationships -
J. Let Your Life Be an Example-

I. Fighting between armed forces.

Verb: act to reduce or prevent something bad or undesirable.

We are fighting forces that are harmful and destructive. We must stop this undesirable behavior and wayward action against people and society. Leadership has a responsibility to act as leaders and become positive difference makers and not selfish destroyers of good.

The fighting never solves the problem; it only enhances the situation and causes more tension between all parties involved. There must be combat multipliers activated through faith, hope, love, mercy, understanding, and grace. Unfortunately, combat takes place under a specific set of rules or be unregulated. When you engage in battle, typically, this means you engage in fighting that involves weapons.

The enemy does not fight fair, especially using coded messages in social media feeds and music. You must know the strategy of chaos through a vindictive messenger.

103

Proverbs 6:34 (NIV)

For jealousy arouses a husband's fury, and he will show no mercy when he takes revenge.

Ezekiel 9:1 (NIV)

Then I heard him call out in a loud voice, "Bring near those who are appointed to execute judgment on the city, each with a weapon in his hand."

II Corinthians 4:8-9 (NLT)

We are pressed on every side by troubles, but we are not crushed. We are perplexed, but not driven to despair. We are hunted down, but never abandoned by God. We get knocked down, but we are not destroyed.

The Power to Overcome:

Succeed in dealing with (a problem or difficulty)

1. Defeat (an opponent); prevail.
2. (Of an emotion) overpower or overwhelm.
3. To get the better in a struggle or conflict.

James 3:13-16 (NLT)

If you are wise and understand God's ways, prove it by living an honorable life, doing good works with the humility that comes from wisdom. But if you are bitterly jealous and there is selfish ambition in your heart, do not cover up the truth with boasting and lying. For jealousy and selfishness are not God's kind of wisdom.

Such things are earthly, unspiritual, and demonic. For wherever there is jealousy and selfish ambition, there you will find disorder and evil of every kind.

Conclusion:

This book is a guide of wisdom against those who possess evil intentions and serve in leadership positions, and they will do anything to stay relevant and in a position of power.

The most important thing is that people will use all avenues of wisdom and substance that God provides daily. I encourage this book's readers to use the insight shared and pattern your life with Godly character, wisdom, and patience. In this hour, we are responsible for ensuring the next generation does not fall victim to leaders whose performance will be low when given such significant positions of power and influence.

Believers of Christ, take your role seriously; souls are looking at you to be an example and beacon of hope for the greater glory of what God has for them. Teach them and empower them for greatness. This is a mandate because you are in a position of trust, authority, responsibility, and confidence.

Share your wisdom and let us rise together to help this generation and the next to know and understand what it means to have success and live a blessed life on the earth for the kingdom of God.

Hungry souls are waiting for revelation and love from the Father and God is looking for a few good soldiers who will lead from the front and not look back.

Matthew 9:36-38 (NLT)
When He saw the crowds, He had compassion on them because they were confused and helpless, like sheep without a shepherd. He said to His disciples, "The harvest is great, but the workers are few. So, pray to the Lord who is in charge of the harvest; ask him to send workers into His fields."

AUTHOR BIO

Dr. Fredrick J. Harris was born in Sumter, South Carolina, on February 4, 1972. Shortly after high school and college, he enlisted in the United States Army. He served with distinction and honor and retired with 26 years of impeccable service to the Nation and is a War Hero & Decorated Combat Veteran. He currently resides near Raleigh, North Carolina, with his wife (Lady) LaKendra, and their sons Marquez, Christian, and Marley.

Apostle Harris joined the United States Army in 1990 and continues to be the leader that God has ordained for him before earth's foundation. He has extensive military training, which has allowed him the opportunity to touch an abundance of Soldiers' lives. His life has touched many in his military tenure and still does. He is a leading example of Christ on earth as he teaches the Soldiers and Believers to follow me as he follows Christ.

Apostle Harris has participated on Ministry Teams on two tours to Iraq 2003 and 2005, and 1 tour to Afghanistan 2012, Glory to God. He has been teaching Bible Study since 2006 in 3 locations Oklahoma, South Carolina, and North Carolina. In November 2009, he was ordained as a Minister at Greenlawn Baptist Church in Columbia, South Carolina. He was a part of an International Bible Study Teaching Institute in France from 2010-2011. In October 2011, he was ordained into Prophetic Ministry at Zoe Ministries New York, NY. In January 2012, he was ordained as Apostle/Prophet/Pastor/Teacher in Greenville, South Carolina. On May 5, 2012, he was ordained and affirmed to Chief Apostle & Founder of Without Limits Fellowship Ministries in Raeford, North Carolina. Apostle Harris was later reaffirmed and consecrated to the Office of Chief Apostle at Faith & Power Christian Center in Dunn, North Carolina.

Apostle Harris is an Apostle of Reconciliation, Peace, and Order with a passion for impacting the world through the Gospel of Jesus Christ. He has traveled to Germany, Kuwait, Ireland, Iraq, Afghanistan, Kyrgyzstan, Belgium, France, Nassau & Freeport Bahamas, and Cozumel Mexico through military and ministerial opportunities to teach and preach the Gospel of Jesus Christ. He has acquired substantial wisdom through life experiences and education. He is the founder of Without Limits Ministries International, Heart of God Embassy, Land of Goshen Outreach Services, and the W.L.M.I. Ministry of Education and Training Academy, located in Raleigh, North Carolina, and 2 Bible Study Ministries, the City of Jerusalem Worship Center and Feet in the Breeze Military Ministry Bible Study with an outreach community Womack Army Hospital Fort Bragg, North Carolina. He is also the Chief Instructor at W.L.M.I. School of Apostolic & Prophetic Ministries, also the W.L.M.I. Prophetic Dream Academy & Mentoring Institute. He has evangelized, ministered, counseled, and taught the Gospel of Jesus Christ to well over 45,000 Soldiers and Civilians in various capacities worldwide.

Education and learning are critical to Apostle Harris as a devout leader in the Body of Christ. He has received his Doctorate in Theology and Christian Education and a Master of Divinity in Christian Counseling from Omni Bible University International. He has received certifications in Military Science and Health Management from (North Central Institute) in Clarksville, Tennessee. Dr. Harris is also certified in Spiritual Empowerment and Resiliency at the (University of Pennsylvania) in Philadelphia, PA. He was honored by the (University of Michigan) and the (National Institute of Mental Health) as a Survey Team Coordinator for successful implementation of the Army S.T.A.R.R.S. (Study to Assess Risk and Resilience in Service Members) Program; conducted studies for ongoing health promotion, risk reduction, and suicide prevention efforts. He is currently pursuing educational opportunities in Network Communications Management. In 2013, Dr. Harris was recommended and selected for a Senior Leader Strategic Fellowship in Interdisciplinary Studies at United States Army Strategic Education, Washington D.C. In (2011) he was awarded a Certificate of Membership by The Fayetteville Cumberland County Ministerial Council.

Dr. Harris became a Certified Christian Life Coach Professional through Freedom Bible College & Seminary in Wilmington, Delaware. His role is to help individuals and clients achieve success in their personal and professional lives in keeping with moral and scriptural foundational truths.

Dr. Harris has recently received accreditation and certification through the North Carolina Academic Association for Private Educators. He has been credentialed and certified by the Association of Christian Schools International. He is currently serving as a Private School Educator in the Middle & High School Academic Departments at New Life Christian Academy & Preparatory School in Fayetteville, North Carolina.

Dr. Fredrick J. Harris is the host of Apostle's Corner Live Stream Broadcast in Raleigh, North Carolina, and the Freedom & Fire T.V./Radio Broadcast in Clinton, North Carolina. These are monthly broadcasts that can be seen and heard worldwide on the airwaves, local cable television, plus the internet through social media platforms of Facebook (Live), YouTube T.V., and Periscope T.V. Apostle's radio talk show is an extension of the W.L.M.I. Outreach Ministry to impact and encourage the community, the Nation, and the world into a closer relationship with The Lord Jesus Christ. Apostle Harris and Lady LaKendra are the Overseers of The Champions for The Lord Prophetic Intercessory Prayer International Virtual Ministry, dedicated to weekly prayer for global outreach ministry work.

Dr. Fredrick J. Harris is a prophetic scribe who has authored several books, manuals, and a stage play. He is the author of "Keep Moving Forward," "Footprints of a King," "The Boomerang Effect," and "God's Grace and A Soldier's Love" (the book and stage play). These anointed resources have given birth to "Kingdom Keys and "M.A.N.N.A. Miraculous Appearance of Necessary Nourishment from The Almighty/Acronyms for Kingdom Building," Fresh Manna for Daily Living, "Embrace Your Moment," "What Happened To Us," "Leadership Gone Rogue," and "Crossroads to Purpose." He has also written several training manuals and curriculum for The W.L.M.I. Apostolic & Prophetic Ministry Training Academy, The Prophetic Dream Academy, The Prophetic Writers & Scribes (The Revealed), and Prophetic Dream Atmospheres & Spiritual Climates training manuals have been implemented into several churches and ministries across the United States and Overseas. He has also authored a 30-day Devotional Impartation Pamphlet Journal to help strengthen people through life coaching tools and personal & spiritual development. His latest accomplishment is the compelling book entitled "Crossroads to Purpose," will galvanize the reader into a personal journey of life through the avenues of music and poetry. Dr. Harris also contributes to ministries, professional marketplace environments, and philanthropy work by writing Letters of Recommendations and contributing to communities through various providential resources. Dr. Harris has assisted with students' and individuals' enrollment and hiring to obtain continuous education at higher learning institutions and professional business workspaces. These include but are not limited to Duke University Divinity School, North Carolina Central University, William Peace University, Fayetteville State University, NC State University, the University of Texas at San Antonio, Bethel Seminary, Colorado Christian University, Duke Health Management, Xerox Recruiting & Management, and Allied Universal Law Enforcement Integration and Training.

Dr. Harris works actively within the community to help promote team building concepts and encourage youth to become tomorrow's leaders. He inspires through coaching sports activities in basketball, soccer, and flag football. Dr. Harris has coached high school basketball and teaches military preparation for service at New Life Christian Academy through the Military Science program. Several young men and women have moved on to play college basketball and service in the United States Military for their chosen branch of service. He continues to educate and empower through his community involvement by mentoring youth and young adults for success in life. Dr. Harris has also certified as a Distance Learning Instructor and Tutor for advanced and higher education. He implements strategies that enable students to personify their talents and learning abilities to build confidence towards their desired educational goals.

Dr. Fredrick J. Harris has been a contributing article writer for Military News with Oasis Montage Magazine in Fayetteville, Georgia. All these anointed aspirations have been birthed out of the heart of God for the people of God. Dr. Fredrick J. Harris is a licensed and ordained Minister, Pastor, Prophet, Apostle, and Prophetic Lecturer. He walks humbly for God in the Apostolic and Prophetic anointing and continues to work in the ministry of God. He gives all honor and praise to our Lord and Savior Jesus Christ for the opportunity to be a servant for the Kingdom of God.

BOOK REVIEW

"A modern-day prophet with the heart, grit, and tenacity reminiscent of the prophet Jeremiah, Dr. Fredrick Harris unrelentingly calls to the task. He holds accountable the object moral, ethical, and social failures of those in leadership positions today.

His uniquely provocative idiom cuts to the core of these failures to reveal a critically urgent admonition resonant of Jeremiah 23, which speaks, "Woe to the shepherds who are destroying and scattering the sheep of my pasture!" declares the Lord.

Leadership Gone Rogue is the bold, audacious modern alarm that echoes Jeremiah's message, "The prophets follow an evil course and use their power unjustly. Both prophet and priest are godless, even in the temple I find their wickedness, declares the Lord."

If you are looking for a body of work that speaks "Truth to Power,"...

THIS IS IT! "

- Dr. Temaki Carr, Apostle-
Loving the Nations
An International Ministry
Fredricksburg, Virginia

Thanks for reading! Please add a short review on

Amazon.com

and let me know what you thought!

BOOK REVIEW

❝❞

"Leadership Gone Rogue provides for anyone who has observed and wondered what has happened to authentic leadership in society the answers from a global perspective. The author, Dr. Frederick J. Harris, exposes the hidden truths of what many people discuss behind closed doors concerning the lack of integrity, honesty, and servitude in leadership.

The author explains in great detail the areas in which leadership is plagued with deception and abuse of power that would cause anyone in any leadership position to reexamine their leadership qualities and skills. The connections between the government, military, church, and individual create a unique yet clear understanding of the importance of accountability in leadership. The distinctions between the government, military, church, and individuals who are using their authority without responsibility are explicitly recognized as a way to answer the proposed question: What has happened to authentic leadership at large?

Those seeking answers in understanding the pitfalls, the cover-ups, and the undeniable ungovern actions that are clearly seen in each spectrum of leadership will be blessed and can use the kingdom principles as solutions for identifying leaderships that have gone rogue."

- Mr. Michael Fulton, Pastor-
Free Will Holy Mission Church
Fayetteville, North Carolina

Thanks for reading!
Please add a short review on Amazon.com and let me know what you thought!

BIBLIOGRAPHY & REFERENCES

1. Leadership Gone Rogue contains research retrieved from Pearson Education, INC., (2007) to generate the context for Page 31.

2. Leadership Gone Rogue contains research retrieved from National Archives, Alpha Omega Publications and School of Tomorrow, (2001 - 2007) to generate the context for Page 32.

3. Leadership Gone Rogue – Chapter 6 - contains Inspiration or themes from the 2010 Film Avengers Initiative 2010 (Iron Man 2).

4. Leadership Gone Rogue – Chapter 7 - contains Inspiration or themes from Colin Powell's 2003 Speech, Weapons of Mass Destruction; before the U.N. Security Council.

5. Leadership Gone Rogue – Chapter 8 - contains Inspiration or themes from Genesis 3:14 and Genesis 1:24 (NIV) Bible Version.

6. Leadership Gone Rogue – Chapter 9 - contains Inspiration or themes from the 2009 Film Angels & Demons- Tom Hanks Movie.

7. Leadership Gone Rogue contains definitions retrieved from Merriam Webster, Free Dictionary.

8. Scriptures marked NCV are ERV are taken from the HOLY BIBLE: EASY-TO-READ VERSION ©2014 by Bible League International. Used by permission.

9. Scriptures marked NCV are ERV are taken from the HOLY BIBLE:

Made in the USA
Columbia, SC
14 March 2021